THE
SLIDING
GLASS DOOR

COLONUS
PUBLISHING

THE SLIDING GLASS DOOR

poems by

SCOTT POOLE

Colonus Publishing Poetry
Colonus Publishing, Inc.
Spokane, Washington

A Colonus Publishing® book
Published by Colonus Publishing, Inc.   www.coloruspublishing.com

Colonus Publishing is the fiction and poetry imprint and a trademark of Colonus Publishing, Inc.

The Colonus Publishing Colophon is a trademark of Colonus Publishing, Inc.

Cover art: Valen © Colonus Publishing, Inc. www.happyartistonline.com
Cover design: Valen © Colonus Publishing, Inc.
Frontispiece: Valen © Colonus Publishing, Inc.
Illustrations pp 64, 65: Valen © Colonus Publishing, Inc.
Photograph of Scott Poole p 67: Monica Smith © Colonus Publishing, Inc.

Interior Design: Glenna Collett
Electronic composition: Glenna Collett
Copy editing: Rich Skalstad

Library of Congress Control Number: 2011931193

Poetry

ISBN: 978-0-0945102-6-9

Printed in the United States of America

Printer: DeHart's Media Services

First edition

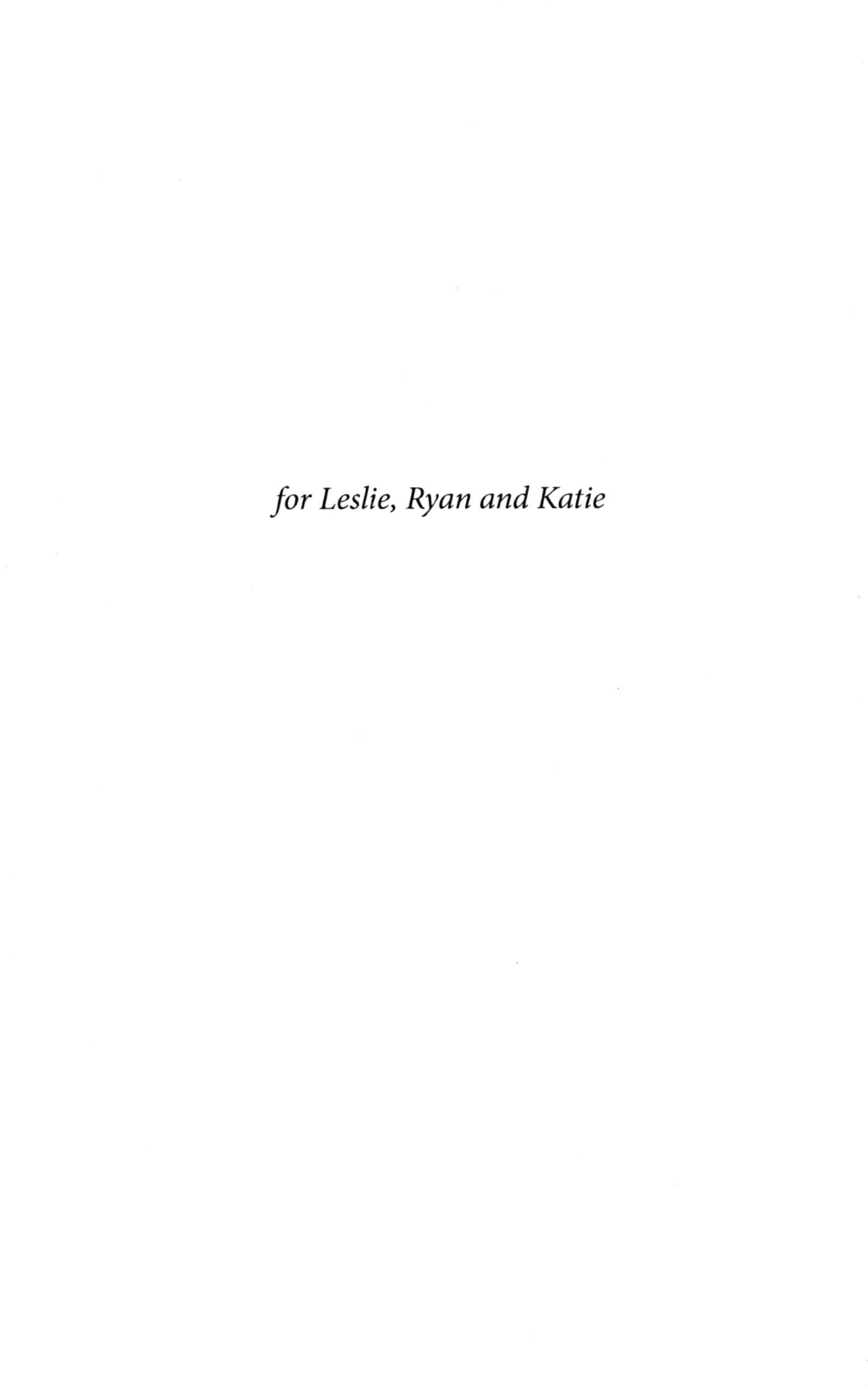

for Leslie, Ryan and Katie

Contents

Why Do You Want to Work Here? 1

Listening to My Wife Wash Dishes 2

How Far Back It Goes 3

1970 4

Somebody's House 6

What Happens Every Year When My Mom Asks Me What I Want for Christmas 7

Argument over the Night Light 9

Aristotle 10

Spokane's Best Chicken Fried Steak 11

By Way of Explanation 12

The Return of Life 14

Flying over Iowa 15

The Beginning of Our Understanding 17

A Beautiful Flower 18

Love Is a Belly Dancer 19

Leak 21

A Little Poem in Celebration of Nothing 22

Thoughts on Chewbacca 24

Our Wonderful Place in History 25

Why? 26

I Want to Believe 28

Lemonade 29

Contents

My House   30

For Alcaeus   32

That's What You Did   34

Small Resistance   35

Encaustic   36

In the Dark, Eyeglasses in Hand   38

What I Will Bring   39

Getting Back   40

The Bible   41

The Small Man   42

At Parties, Talking to the Insane   43

Everyone Wants Me to Write a Poem about Santa Claus   44

My Name Is Gilbert Scobee   46

Keeping the Promise   47

A Brief History of America   49

The Cement World Beats the Non-Cement World   50

I Was a Cubicle   51

Visit from a Bullfighter   52

How Our Living Room Became a Cemetery   54

Heaven   55

Shelving   56

Folding Chairs   57

Gentle Majesty   58

Can't Sleep   60

Dying Wishes   61

How Good It Feels to Die   63

Why Do You Want to Work Here?

Well, I was just up above, not thinking of much,
flying overhead in my puttering biplane,
enjoying a temporary airy existence of light,
silence, and unlimited hope, bound only by
fluffy clouds, horizon, and the occasional magnificent
mountain peak, when my engine suddenly burst into flames.

That's when I first became intrigued by the work of your company.
Well, more specifically the largely unobstructed orange color
of your company's roof.
Despite dragging a tremendous column of black smoke,
I spiraled down from ten thousand feet
in a somewhat controlled gyre before
coming to the softest kiss of an emergency landing
that you've ever seen
over a fulfillment department.

It was such a beautiful touchdown
that I was able to walk down your backstairs,
through receiving, past packing and right into
the velvety cubic walls of your human resources office
without so much as a single protest.

It's that kind of welcoming attitude
that I can really appreciate in a company
that may or may not have fire insurance.
May I put my scarf and goggles on your desk?
Champagne?

Listening to My Wife Wash Dishes

Oh, I know what you're thinking—
How typical. The wife has to wash the dishes
and you're off writing some damn poem
while she does all the work in the house
and I bet you don't even have your shoes on
and your pants stink and you expect her
to wait on you hand and foot
like some kind of slave.

I really don't care if that's what you're thinking,
because it won't change the fact that the sound
of my wife doing the dishes
is one of the most beautiful
and comforting sounds in the world.
It just is.

And before you go jumping to conclusions,
condemning every one of my poems, maybe
I was only listening to her on a tape recorder
because she died
several years ago after a tragic accident
trying to save giant pandas in China.
And after you've heard the sound of a loved one
being brutally mauled and ripped apart by a giant panda,
the sound of that same someone simply washing some dishes
is pretty damn amazing. Did you ever think of that? Huh?

So why don't you back off on the fairness radar for a sec
so that for the love of giant pandas and all the holy people trapped
    in the clouds
I can just finish this goddamn poem already.

Wishy, wishhy, screech, scrich, wishhy, wish, swish . . .

How Far Back It Goes

The salamander falls off the leaf
and drifts down the side of a deep
canyon into the wild dark
of a lazy mountain stream
and begins sucking on the side of a rock
that no man will ever touch or ever care to.
Then some sort of deep, disturbed fish
comes up and kisses the ass of the salamander.
Then some other horrible aquatic creature,
something no person living or dead
has ever seen, kisses the ass of that fish.
The ass kissing continues through the afternoon,
deep, way back into the dark crags of history,
into the very fathomless evil
that no person will ever understand.
Kissing asses goes that far back, that deep.
Now here in a kitchen in the middle of the plain day
you give me an honest hug and say thank you.
I love that I have no idea what it's for.

1970

I love people born in 1970,
like me.
You can see it in their eyes.
Well, I can see it in their eyes.
There's a knowledge there,
a brilliance.
Everyone born in 1970 is brilliant.
But not a lot of people know this.
Everyone born in 1970 is a bad promoter
of his own talents.
People born in 1970 hate 1969.
Everybody knows that.
1969 took up everything.
1970 is like the day after a prom
when people are dressed normal again
and meet at 7-11 and feel stupid
and hate their pathetic lives.
Bebe Rebozo was featured on the cover of *Life* the week I was born.
No one born in 1970 knows who the hell Bebe Rebozo is.
They just like the fact that bozo is part of his last name.
There are no organizations available
to help people born in 1970.
Doesn't that show a lack of respect?
People born in 1970 really like trees, evergreen trees,
you know, the big tall kind.
They will stare at them for hours
when they could be vigorously promoting an agenda for a better
    America.
Everyone born in 1970 lives in Vancouver, Washington.
Everyone born in 1970 lies.
Of course, these are all gross overgeneralizations.
Everyone, I mean everyone born in 1970
can't get enough of gross overgeneralizations.
But when I say everyone,

I'm just talking about myself again.
Everyone born in 1970 talks about himself too much
then worries about it all day
but at the same time doesn't do a damn thing.
So maybe that's the problem.
I don't know.
You figure it out.

Somebody's House

This looks like somebody's mom's house.
Not my mom's house
but somebody's mom's house.
She could be in there giving birth right now,
not my mom, of course, but somebody's.
But it doesn't look like somebody's mom is home,
so she must be at the hospital
where a mom becomes a mom.
But the hospital is not anyone's mom's house,
it's everyone's mom's house for a little while,
until she goes back to a house,
and it could be this one—it could be your mom's house.
But it's not my mom's house. It's somebody's,
somebody's who could be a mom
at her own house, but not my house.
Somebody's mom probably forgot to call somebody to say
that she's a mom or she bought a house,
not this house but somebody's.

What Happens Every Year When My Mom Asks Me What I Want for Christmas

I say, "You know, Mom, I just want everyone to be happy,
happy like holding a balloon on a sunny day in a park,
while playing a banjo.
I want everyone to be happy playing a banjo
with yellow balloons tied to its tuning pegs, standing in a park.
That's all.

"Just think, if everyone we knew, knew how to play banjo,
think what fun that would be. We could have banjo playing parties
where people drank punch playing banjos, danced around in city
        parks
playing the banjo, and if suddenly attacked
by a party crasher or a wild animal,
we could beat them down with our handy banjos
and strangle them with the strings of our yellow balloons.

"Except nobody I know, including myself,
knows how to play the banjo. So I guess I'd like to get some banjo
        lessons
if you don't mind. Please buy me some banjo lessons so I can
teach everyone I know and give back to the community.

"And some fencing lessons, too, I think,
so I could wield my banjo like a giant lollipop of death.
And really, if you wouldn't mind, about 150 yellow balloons to go
        with that,
no wait, camouflage balloons that I would tie to my extremities
so I would look like an innocent, slick, and bulbous arborvitae
secreted in the night in front of the rec hall,
ready to pounce on any steely interlopers
trying to annihilate our banjo hootenanny.

"Really, if this works for you, Mom,
I'd like to train an elite team of banjo warriors
who could be dispatched at any minute to any corner of the globe,
floating about the planet in yellow balloon death ships of happiness
with rockets on them and giant speakers blaring 'Foggy Mountain
        Breakdown'
who could swoop down on any depressed population, deluging
        them
with spontaneous banjo concerts and yellow balloon giveaways
and, of course, bludgeon any party poopers
with a frenetic flurry of banjo whacking.

"So I think I'm going to need a secret lair powered by a nuclear
        reactor,
a six million gallon tank of helium, some used airliner parts, 2,523
        banjos,
a secret banjo martial arts dojo, and a couple of boxes of Sharpies
so we can paint happy faces on our yellow balloons
and the dead foreheads of anyone who would seek to crush our
        merriment."

"How about a shirt?" she replies. "Shirts are nice."

Argument over the Night Light

Thomas Alva Edison had 14 cows,
but his wife took care of them
while he was off inventing things
up to 18 hours a day
after he retired at the age of 75.
So what?
Why didn't he just stay home
with his 15 damn kids
and 14 damn cows?
Who needs the light bulb
anyway, and the phonograph,
and the movies? (I can't go
because I have to watch my kids.)
He pretty much destroyed
mystery and darkness
and now my kids
scream for the night light,
and all their electric toys beep,
knocking stars out of the night
with the batteries he invented.
It's all his damn fault
because he never had the balls to stay home
and deal with his family.
So screw you, Thomas Alva Edison.
"Yes, honey," I say.
"I'll find your night light right away."

Aristotle

I was in one of those Jiffy Lube
six-by-six waiting rooms,
picking at my crack, when
I noticed a bald man with a long white beard
staring at me while I tried
to relieve the itching
through persistently unwieldy layers
of denim, cotton, and rain jacket material.
I thought: This guy looks just like Aristotle.
What if this is Aristotle,
a man who decided that everything
in the universe should be pigeon-holed,
cubbied, stuffed, and jammed into
its own singular definition
so that an average guy of average mind
may be able to understand the vagaries
of the universe through
the routine categorizations of daily life?
That was really nice of him to think of all that.
I hoped I wasn't insulting his theories
but instead proving them to be true somehow
by picking my butt in a Jiffy Lube.
Obviously, Aristotle is dead,
but at least it took my mind off
the itching for a moment.
Thanks Aristotle.

Spokane's Best Chicken Fried Steak

I'm choking,
and now
nearly all my fingers are down my throat,
which is actually not helping much
in the breathing department,
and the tragedy of this situation
is that I choked because I was shocked
that I had left my keys in my car
along with my cell phone,
and I sucked in all the nearby air
and every living creature in it.
I'm not sure what is down there,
but I'm patting my chest
like I'm looking for an underwear drawer
I can pull open
to release the ball of socks stuck in my lung.
Anyway, a car has stopped at the stoplight now
out here in front of the parking lot
and I can hear from its radio an advertisement
for a restaurant announcing "Spokane's Best Chicken Fried Steak."
I try to wave to them
but they drive off fast.
Meanwhile, people are at a diner somewhere
thinking to themselves:
This isn't "Spokane's Best Chicken Fried Steak."
It may be second,
but it sure as hell ain't the first.
Then they light up cigarettes
and stare long and without purpose
at the passing traffic.

By Way of Explanation

I was driving up the freeway exit ramp
and a cardboard sign
in a man's hand
read: "Please help, Scott."

First, I thought
you're kind of limiting your options.
I mean how many Scotts
could there possibly be
that might drive by?

What if your name
was Pepe
and you had raging case of altruism?

But then I thought
this man's name is Scott
and he just wants you to know
who you are giving to.

That's brilliant.
A personal touch.
This guy is a pro.

But then it occurred to me
he might be asking for help
for me, Scott.

And I thought
that's really, really nice of him.
Nobody asked him to collect help for me.

And I suddenly realized
that maybe I could use a helping hand
and I didn't even know it.

I looked up to the heavens
and thanked them
for bringing this special soul
into my dismal day

and that's
when I accidentally
ran him over with my car.

The Return of Life

Boarding the bus at 7 a.m., I notice,
instead of the usual death pallor,
all the old men are talking at once,
excited, joyful, and fully interested
about how to take a bus uptown.

I'm thoroughly scared until I see her—
spiked high heels, long legs of gold,
a black skirt, a perfect suit,
large breasts, spiked blond hair—
all encompassed in a cloud of perfume
40 ft. in circumference.

I sit down behind her.
"What do you do for a living?" blue stocking cap asks her.
"I work for a mortgage company."
"So you're the one who repossesses everything?"
asks the man in the shiny black shoes.
"Yes, that's me," she says.

The men and bus are suddenly quiet.
And it's true, sitting there calmly
in the molten morning sun
pouring in with the blue eternal horizon,
she is repossessing everything.

Flying over Iowa

Hey, we're flying over Iowa.
Well, actually Minnesota.
No, I think it's Kentucky.
It can't be Kentucky.
I think it's the highlands of Wisconsin.
This is Illinois. See that brown patch—
that's where Bob's cousin Louise
once divorced great uncle Seymour
near a Sycamore tree in a grove
by the river that flows out of Oklahoma.
That's too far south,
and nothing flows out of Oklahoma,
not on my watch.
Well, look at that cloud—it looks a lot like
Michigan.
So?
So it's a cloud that looks like . . .
That doesn't look like Michigan,
that's Pennsylvania if anything.
Where's Philly then? That hole?
Yes, if that's how you want to put it,
that hole, that's where Philly is.
No wonder the doughnut was invented there.
The doughnut wasn't invented in Philly.
Where then?
Hamburg, I think.
What?
Hamburg, Germany.
That's the home of the hamburger not the doughnut, you idiot.
The hamburger was the precursor
of the doughnut. The first hamburgers were made
on white bread with holes cut in them. That's where
you put the condiments and wondered about
all the holes in your life—

holes of time and love and happiness
and how you might fill them
and with what magic condiment.
That's stupid.
Well, it's the truth,
and I don't care what you say.
That hole is not Philadelphia.

The Beginning of Our Understanding

Steam rises from a pile of scrambled eggs
the size of the hot tub in their back yard.
"We used over eight hundred eggs," they tell us.
This is what you can expect from the recently unemployed:
the handiwork of free time.
They invited everyone they knew.
I was chicken. I was insulted. I didn't talk,
drank screwdrivers, and threw rocks into the eggs
when no one was looking.
Finally, a woman caught me but didn't turn me in.
She just turned me on.
"Wouldn't you love to make love in those eggs?"
"Maybe they already have," I said.
"What a way to share your life with your friends."
"Remember when we were little
no one wanted to share? Now people
want to share too much and in all the wrong ways."
She smiled and disrobed. She was stunning.
No one noticed her because they were too busy looking
at the giant pile of disgusting eggs.
We clinked our glasses. Smiled.
It was the beginning of our understanding.

A Beautiful Flower

Don't call her vagina a beautiful flower.
Please don't.
If her vagina were a beautiful flower
then she would have bees in her pants all the time,
and it would be impossible to hold her
close enough to be intoxicated
by the gossamer tendrils of her perfume.
One cannot be swept away by subtle drops of dew
welling at the corners of her eyes
when you reveal your most vulnerable,
most baby-chick-soft sentiments,
if your dearest love is hopping around
like a River Dancer on crack,
waving her hands madly in front of her crotch.
Then all you've got is a screaming freak-out
ripping her pants off in public,
and that would not be a flower, my friend.
That would be porn.

Love Is a Belly Dancer

Love can be, well, lovely,
silken, golden,
a simple star of hope
coming from the ancient void,
a rare and many-faceted jewel
encrusted in the belly button
of a sweaty belly dancer
at a questionable Lebanese restaurant
with even more questionable food
that is already making
your intestines gyrate
before you are even done
with the couscous
on a Thursday night
when you decided to go out
even though you knew
a night eating at home
would be better than
some sketchy Lebanese restaurant
in a strip mall and that
if you stayed home
you might have had
a perhaps .05 percent chance
that in a fit of passion
you and your life's love
would have just said to hell with it
and smashed the dinner plates
and had experimental sex
featuring several here-to-now
undiscovered positions
right there on the kitchen table
but now you're just worried
your glass of water
won't be refilled,

the same water that is taking
on an orange and green hue
as the swirling, sweaty
center of the belly
draws nearer, the dollar bills
in her waist band fanning
your quickly drying eyes.

Leak

Under her car
in search of the cat
no moonlight shines off
oil dripping

from the broken
pan onto my arm
and it appears
as if I'm injured

and the fluid
is as warm as blood
when it escapes
and runs from

the heart to places
we never thought
we would go for love
or the loss of it.

A Little Poem in Celebration of Nothing

Nothing traumatic happened today,
nothing interesting either.
I had some coffee.
My left eye was ominous in the gleam of the butter knife.
I don't know if anybody was afraid
but I think I scared the hell out of the butter.
My hands ran down the sliding glass door, smearing it.

I went and found the glass cleaner,
spritzed down the windows, and the glass was clean.
Then I palmed it.
I spritzed it again and cleaned it again.
Then I marked it up again.

This went on for about an hour . . . .
A bird flew across the sky.
Not that this is a unique occurrence.
Not that this hasn't happened before.

Then I noticed two people fucking in the backyard.
They were energetic in their motions,
animals on the edges of time, performing
the rituals from which they were born.

There wasn't anyone fucking in the backyard.
I just made that up.
There was some grass growing, though.
"How infinitely pleasing this is," Whitman might say.
Well, I'm not so sure. I'll have to look that up.

Getting dark now and it's quiet.
The calm is its own castle.
Did Rilke say that? Maybe.
I think I'm going to lie and say
now I made a Braunschweiger sandwich,
yes, with mustard and onions.

Thoughts on Chewbacca

Lying in bed this morning, wondering why
I didn't die mercifully in my sleep,
I wanted to cry out—I wanted to cry out like Chewbacca.

Sometimes, I wish I had only one thing to say.
People would ask, "How are you doing?" or
"Could you do me a favor?" and all I could say is
"Hmmhmmmhmmwwwhhhwmmmmeeeemhhhweeemhhh."
And that would be enough. Some would even pretend
to know what I'm talking about.

How beautiful is Chewbacca's cry: part whine,
part existential resignation, and mostly indecipherable
to those not hip enough to understand.

I imagine myself as Chewbacca sometimes
when I'm lying on the living room floor watching television.
I would look just like a bad rug from the '70s
(which I can imagine was the original inspiration for the character).
I would love to be hidden in plain sight. How nice that would be.

Then as everyone is settled into their program,
after all the guests have been served their drinks,
I'd jump up on my own terms, at my own time,
and let fly with a melodic and soulful
"Hmmhmmmhmmwwwhhhwmmmmeeeemhhhweeemhhh."

Then maybe people might know,
as the drinks fly and the screams ring out,
they might really know
what it feels like to be a beautiful carpet,
hopeful of walking on something
besides yourself.

Our Wonderful Place in History

We are as important as steak
sizzling on a brontosaurus.

How wonderful to see the non-caring look
on that brontosaurus as he gazes
at the small burning object on his back
then chomps down a palm tree.

The pathetic piece of cow
cries for attention
but the brontosaurus turns and eats again
another tree and then another.

At him I throw slice after slice
of spiral-cut ham
and piece after piece
of hickory mountain bacon,
T-bones, ham hocks, flank steaks, pork chops,
but now he is ignoring me.

My sidekick, Herbie,
declares, "He's an herbivore like me.
Meat will get you nowhere."
"No. No. This will work," I say,
launching fifty pound sausage patties
onto his back. They land
with the loud, wet thuds
of a low production horror movie,
but still he ignores me.

Bored, the brontosaurus rumbles
his thirty metric tons
away from us, eating a swath,
stinking meat hanging from his sides,
leaving us to consider
our important place in history.

Why?

Why should I get up tomorrow
or tie my shoes? Who cares?
Why look for eggs to fry
or even some horrible cereal to eat?

People everywhere call it quits all the time.
Why can't I for a while? Depression.
An American past time, blah, blah, whatever.

It's how you drop out that's important.
Maybe you lie on the floor naked,
slowly trying to kill yourself
by eating too many bananas.

The phone is ringing now
and it's not like you're going to get up
because you're working on your thirtieth banana
and maybe you can't even talk,
your throat bloated
by too much banana eating.

Perhaps this sort of thing leads to
an enormous growth of fur,
your skin turning darker as the sun
heats you to mush.

The phone rings several more times
through the next several days and finally
someone smashes through the door.
The smell hits the rescue party
as if a zoo went horribly wrong.

You're nothing but a writhing mass of banana peels
in the middle of the floor with a pair of legs.
It takes all they've got
to pull you out by the ankles and drag you out the door into the yard
to ask you questions. You can't answer.
You use sign language.
But no one there understands sign language.

You're trying to explain Wittengstein's
theory of meaning
as a social event
using sign language
to a room of staring EMTs.

Oh, look at that.
You've defecated on the grass.
That's not going to help your case.

No matter. They clean it up.
They shower you and tuck you
into a clean white bed
and you take a nice wonderful nap,

and when you finally feel like you want to work
because you feel like a king,
like a captain of industry,
like you want to run a company,
cure a disease,
be the mayor,
or win a gold medal in the Olympics,

you're restrained.
Screw Wittengstein.
This food ain't too bad.

I Want to Believe

Weren't there 14 holes in some gangster,
some famous gangster with 14 holes?

But he wouldn't die, despite
the sudden streams of blood running from him.

He kept firing despite all the holes,
and it so shocked the police that they

just stopped and let him empty his clips
willy-nilly into the barriers they were

hiding behind with their bulletproof
helmets and vests and genital cups

and shivering coffee in shatterproof mugs,
wearing every piece of protective clothing imaginable

while he fired round after round.
Didn't they just wait for him to drop?

Didn't he just stand there waiting
for a response for over ten hours?

Oh, I hope so.
I hope I didn't just make that up.

Lemonade

One time
when I sold lemonade

I sold it for ten dollars
instead of ten cents.

Yes, you guessed it,
I didn't sell a single Dixie cup

but got a lot of attention.
Everyone wanted a sample

even though it was cold and cloudy,
but I refused.

I was locked on ten dollars.
After they left confused

because they couldn't afford me,
I drank all the lemonade myself

and it was the best, the best
thousand dollars I never made.

My House

It's the weekend. A Saturday.
There are three children sleeping
in the rooms of my house.
My son. My daughter. My nephew. My house.
I'm in charge. Me.
It's 9:16 p.m. in the dark days of October.
Rain pounds the house, and the porch light,
as I peer out, fills with breath.
Yesterday, one of the top five
people in the White House was
indicted for perjury. A man named Scooter.
I have almost constant rib pain now,
but I'm not being indicted for perjury.
No great scandal is rocking my house.
I took my high blood pressure medication
and my thyroid medication.
I have three beautiful children
sleeping in my three bedroom house,
with two and half baths
and a kitchen complete with a kitchen island.
Today I took the children to tour
a submarine sitting in the Willamette River.
Sometimes I wonder that randomness
such as this is allowed.
Then we watched a laser light show. Wow!
And we drove home through the rain.
Washington State lost to USC 13 to 54.
The neighbor took the kids for two hours while I cleaned.
It was beautiful. I actually cleaned.
I was on my knees in the kitchen with a wash cloth.
The whole day was beautiful.
My sister brought over her 8-month-old.
When your house is clean and people
gladly bring you their children

and everyone trusts you while they're
out getting religion or drunk or laid,
life can be an unbelievable miracle.
The president can kiss my ass.
Everyone can come live with me.

For Alcaeus

Thanks Alcaeus for the Alcaic stanza.
I thought someone should say it.
I didn't care about you until I heard your story.

Oh, to be hated by a Lesbian tyrant named Pittacus,
kicked off Lesbos,
forced to swim the Mediterranean,
salt water stinging your scratched testicles.

I can't even imagine
trying to swim in a chiton.
My God!
It must have been like
making love to curtains
without the rod.

Then, to have only a few poems
survive the stinking years.

Alcaeus, all the encyclopedia
will tell me is that you invented
a certain kind of poetic meter
and that you were disappointed,

to say the least, about poor Lesbos,
that you hated tyrants (who doesn't?)
and that you always said
a little love and a lot of wine goes a long way.
You were Aphrodite right about that.

Today, Alcaeus,
I heard a song by Crosby, Stills, and Nash,
and it reminded me that
David Crosby gave his semen
freely to lesbians
in Marin County, California,
around the turn of the millennium.

Sing with me Alcaeus! The music rises.
The chorus joins in ever so gently.
We want to be your friend.
What have you got to lose?

That's What You Did

She held small perfumed rocks in her hand
to throw at a clown
because it was the thing to do
in 1926 when there was helium
and respiration and people with names
like Buzz and Elijah danced things
with names like the Lindy and the Foxtrot
and when the flood broke the levy
everyone had work clothes to put on.
There was no shortage of heroes
because almost everyone had lost a child
to childbirth and so a flood
of water was just another of life's
cruelties that made the calm moments sweeter
than they've been since 1926
when planes were still a novelty
and boys had books on their beds
and looked out the window and pointed
and it was some sort of rule
that you knew what make and model and year
every car was and the factory it was made in.
And chances are you had an uncle who worked in a factory
and whistled at women, and they still thought
this sort of thing was sexy,
and right over his shoulder was a church
where little girls were playing and throwing
handfuls of gravel at a clown
who had been paid a $1.50
for the afternoon because that's what
you did: torture clowns
in your pretty white dress
back in 1926 before the floods came.

Small Resistance

I walked out to the yard
and pulled up some grass today,
just like I'd done for a week.
I wanted to feel that small resistance
before the earth lets go.

Then I gave the wasted blades
back to the ground.

In grief it seems so dramatic,
but think of golfers casually
testing wind with grass
before receiving oversized checks.

Think of farmers pulling it up
and rolling it between fingers
as if miracles could come from it.

Think of children
ripping out handfuls as they roll
laughing across the lawn.

Think how it seems the earth
always grows enough
to say, "Here, my child, more."

But I know all is not forgiven
because there still is this resistance,
this smallest fight
like the one I felt
taking off your lapel pin
before they lowered you in.

Encaustic

Forget about organization.
The amber sunset makes me
want to pour wax over it all,
even the front of my kitchen pantry,
seal it up for good and start over,
trap the rotting cases of beans from Walmart,
that dried fruit we'll never eat,
the city blocks of Rice-A-Roni,
and the tuna fish which refuses to die
next to the bags of dumbstruck egg noodles.

Why stop there?
I'm going to pour wax over that damn blackberry bush
over by the rusty blue fence in the backyard,
watch those berries turn a perfect mottled black.
Just for good measure I'm going to take my socks off
and throw them into the mix. Have you ever truly
flung your socks into a blackberry bush?
Just go out and do it right now. You'll see.

That's fine. I'll stop the poem for you.

Well, don't listen to me, but I'll tell you a little secret:
When you fling an old pair of wool monkey socks
onto a blackberry bush, all the berries drop off at once.
Not only that, each blackberry splits into black balls
and rearranges back into its molecule of choice. It's true.

What molecule would you rearrange into?
And what are your favorite elements?
Strontium? Californium? Zinc?

Don't you love the Periodic Table of Elements?
Don't you love the square shelves of it?
Don't you love the font?

The universal pantry. Let's pour wax over it, too,
until each element is like a kitchen window on a rainy day,
steamed from making spaghetti, or a square
of golden linoleum too hard to look past,
or something finally solid and beautiful enough
to hang on the wall forever.

In the Dark, Eyeglasses in Hand

This is the moment
no one paints,
no one sculpts.
This is the forgotten moment.
No photograph in the dark.
No flash
of forgiveness.
This is the moment
of garbage can lids under snow,
topics not discussed,
drama not ready-made.
No textbook can do justice
to this momentum
of bone suspended in skin.
The talk of nerves
following the path of prayers.
Unseen water streams over rocks.
While other passengers sleep
a man wakes on a train
traveling two parallel lines
through the shuddering dark
toward a star
just perfecting the horizon.

What I Will Bring

If we ever talk again
and have a little conversation,
I'll bring the conversation piece.

What should it look like?
A duck? A baked halibut?
Venus carved in pimento loaf?

Should it be orange? An orange kangaroo?
Is the color of mistrust
magenta on a rainy day?

Should it smell like a dinosaur
lumbering from a swamp
or the simple forgiveness of daisies?

Should it feel like a rifle in the snow,
sticking your finger inside cornbread,
a cat's tongue on wet grass?

Will it be silent or softly wail
through the words that fall from us like dust
on a dark table without sound.

What taste will it leave in your mouth
after we're done with our conversation?
What will you say to bring me back?

Getting Back

My child's macaroni and cheese
rotting on a brown plate
reminds me of wet logs
in a lumber yard
14 miles deep in the forest,
awaiting collection
in the hills that pile into
the long running valleys
of dusk covered mountains,
places only the local men know,
the men who search through piles
of maps in their basements,
piles of maps everyone wants them
to throw into a landfill somewhere,
but they know keeping the maps is important,
especially the large, rolled-up maps,
the kind you can set on the dining room table
and spread with both hands
like you are making a bed,
smoothing the world to two dimensions,
the kind you can point at and say,
"This is where we did it,
right here."

The Bible

Just in case.
It's over there.

Because you have to have at least one.
The part I read the most
is the inscription
to my wife's grandmother.

I imagine God at a book signing,
signing her copy,
"Dear Eva, thanks for worshipping."

But mainly I consider when
she may have held it in her hands:

a few times at church,
a couple of confused moments in the bedroom,
and one strange time after mass

when she walked to the grocery store
and set it for a few seconds
on a stack of apples
while she inspected the bananas for bruises.

The Small Man

The small man crawls
from his lunchbox.
He has decided to climb out
and admire the art on the side.
After all, it's a Cézanne
and how often do you see
a Cézanne on the side of a lunchbox
early in the day
when everyone is off working
or napping or maybe passively
searching a grocery aisle?
There are only so many giant candy bars
you can consider, only so much beautiful
Wonder Bread you can nap on.
One must do something
with the day besides carving Cheetos.
It's the climb
to the edge of the lunchbox
that is his favorite part,
looking over the edge
of his metal wall,
swinging the foot over,
the transition from meal
to musing,
the colors of the Cézanne
rising like heat.

At Parties, Talking to the Insane

The insane man opens his mouth
and inside is an easel.

The other people eat cheese and talk
and congratulate each other.

Pines with cones painted just off the branches.
A deer stares at its feet in the river.

A hiker walks the space between the mountain
and the mountain top. "I want to be the first
to snap a picture of a mountain's underbelly," he says.

An apple separates from its stem.

The fish swim upside-down in the river,
their tails already in the ocean.

"I don't want to go home," I say,
"because I'm listening to this painting, my dear."

I pull out my tweezers and approach the insane man.
Like a hungry baby bird I take the small painting.

"Thank you," he says, and rises to join the others.

Everyone Wants Me to Write a Poem about Santa Claus

Really, you don't want a poet to write a poem about Santa Claus.
Poets can't be trusted with this sort of responsibility.
A poet-created Santa Claus would ride in on an unicycle,
dressed head to toe in brown tweed with a fake Walt Whitman
    beard.
He'd be towed on a ski rope by a giant flying sturgeon named
    Randolph.
Santa would always travel underground like the simple worm,
metaphorically stamping himself with the plight of the common
    man
and instead of the chimney, he would
come up from the basement
like the rebirth of dandelions in the spring—
which makes more sense when you think about it,
and he would leave little dishes of caviar
scattered about on elegant crackers,
because this was the thing in 1853
to set under the Christmas tree,
and Santa doesn't like to update his act
being nothing but a hopelessly unpractical romantic.
And he wouldn't say ho, ho, ho. He would say
"Happy brief reprieve in the nightmare of human existence!"—
a line he borrowed from a British poet no one can remember.
At this point he would throw the traditional Christmas dictionary
at the tree, and it would turn into a leafless winter maple.
Then at the fore-chosen time to distribute the wealth of gifts,
Santa would handwrite 102 traditional witty couplets
and tie one to each bare branch of the maple.
All his traditional tasks done, he would then
steal every bit of food in the house and feed it to the sturgeon
(an ironic reminder of the gluttony of the holiday).
Finally, accompanied by a tremendous belch from Randolph,
Santa would replace all the gas in your car
with eggnog, jump around in a circle three times,
and ride his unicycle back into the basement.

Instead of wanting Santa Claus to land on your shingles
you would avoid him like a case of the shingles.
Instead of Christmas lights in your yard,
you would build elaborately decorated
geodesic domes with gun slits and steel-lined floors
to try to keep Santa out.
Your biggest traditional act of the season would be
praying to Jesus as hard as you could
that Santa would just leave you alone this year.

My Name Is Gilbert Scobee

This time I dump my first twenty girlfriends
instead of them dumping me.
This time my name is Gilbert Scobee.
I'm sitting in a gray room
in Jackson, Mississippi,
not even aware it's the home town
of Eudora Welty,
and I'm trying to sell a mortgage
to any sucker I can find
on that gorgeous Internet that stretches wide
like thighs always do for me
because I'm selling mortgages
and my name is Gilbert Scobee
and I'm not even aware that
I'm trying to sell the mortgages
to my former self, Scott Poole,
the one who did get dumped
by his first twenty girlfriends,
the one who writes poetry now,
not someone important like me
who writes credit plans,
whose name is Gilbert Scobee,
and wears aftershave
and God bless the Internet because no one,
not even my former self,
can smell it this far away.

Keeping the Promise

I am a man committed to watching his children.
My children are committed to watching me.
We watch each other and commit frequently.

Are others out there committing as equally?
They might be. Some dad might be my equal.
I wonder if we could go out and compare notes?

Maybe get a cup of coffee, sit and talk awhile.
Examine each other's habits so that we could
commit even more to our children. Perhaps

other dads like myself could get together
for a three week retreat in the Rocky Mountains,
skiing, skeet shooting, and bear wrestling

just to discuss how committed to our children
we are. We'd need a lot of time, so no kids allowed.
Of course we'd need weekly meetings

and encounter groups and we could role play,
one group of us pretending to be children
and the other group pretending to be fathers.

In fact, we could role play for an entire year
around the clock, 24/7 until we get it right.
Yes, then we would make no mistakes

with our own kids. In fact, if I didn't have kids
that would even be better. Cardboard kids
I could always commit to and still get to my

committing meetings and not have to worry
about giving them constant commitment. That's it!
I'm going to have sex with a cardboard box.

I'll put my entire self in a cardboard box,
commit in my mind as hard as I can,
and someday they'll mail me to my children.

A Brief History of America

I like the little Coke bottles
the best. The six and a half ounce ones,
the ones with the lazy French curves,
the woman-with-hips look to them,
the old kind, the kind
our grandfathers carried down
country lanes while waving
to each other as they passed
on the way to the market
to sell their hand-grown vegetables
and homemade wares.

The plastic bottles will do.
We have to accept plastic as modern citizens,
so I sip from the plastic, dreaming
of the glass, which seem
so much more refreshing,
but we can't have everything
and bottles are a mere footnote
in life's diary.

The can is the worst, though.
All I want to do is chug it,
crush it, and hurl it across the street
at some poor son of a bitch.
I'd like to see him just try and yell at me
as the metal hunks of cars
rip through the air fast enough
to take your breath away.

The Cement World Beats the Non-Cement World

The old man had a billy goat he would often take to market.
This billy goat made many a villager jealous,
for it was the most elegant of all billy goats, the Cadillac of goats.

Its hoofs were like the shiniest spinning rims.
The fur on its side had the beautiful sheen
of the finest polished chrome.
One sight of it eating mangoes and women would swoon.
The old man would park the billy goat diagonally in the barn
and next to it, would lay out its halter and feed bucket.

There was a small sign explaining the year the goat was born
and his lineage extending deep into the grandfather of all goats.
This goat's ancestors were once owned by kings.

"Where did he get that killer goat?" the other villagers would say.
Some would spend too much time admiring the old man's goat.
Some divorces ensued. Some families were broken.
Such was the sad attraction of this royal goat.

Soon the whole village began falling apart.
Everyone was in a general malaise.
No matter how hard they tried,
they couldn't have the old man's goat,
and soon they forgot the point of living.

Women at the peak of their lives jumped off the bridge,
and everyone in the village blamed the old man for the women's
    deaths.
Because there were no more child-bearing women in the village,
no more children were born.

Soon the village was emptied, and the old man was forced
to parade his goat around his yard, which endlessly pleased him,
because he could kick the goat now, without the worry of jealous
    eyes.

I Was a Cubicle

The day before yesterday, I was a cubicle. I was hired with a team of three other people to hold hands around the desk of Andrew Rutherford. I got the job through one of the temp agencies. We were required to wear these really bulky sandwich boards. Luckily, I didn't have to wear the one with the shelves on it containing the dusty computer software boxes. Tina drew that straw and was none too happy about it. She kept complaining about her shoulder aching the whole day, and I have to tell you I think Andrew was getting a bit ticked around 2 p.m. because he just left and came back with every edition of C, C+, C++ and C# for Dummies and dropped them on her shelf. We had been trying to shush her all day, but in the end she paid the price. Around 3:30 she just collapsed and destroyed Andrew's computer, the left side of his desk, and I think one of his ribs. He was really screaming. We all tried to come to their aid, but all we achieved was crushing the two of them under the weight of our sandwich boards and destroying office productivity for the rest of the day. Tomorrow I've been reassigned to putting foam on hangers with the mentally challenged.

Visit from a Bullfighter

I show him the croquet set.
It's broken. Nobody has played in years.
Next, we turn on the television to find a show

but he stabs his sword straight through it.
So I show him the beer in the fridge.
It's cheap. It's cold. He declines.

"Do you want to play Scrabble?" I ask.
"Do you have Scrabble?" he replies.
"No," I answer. He says nothing.

In my Subaru, I drive him to the waterfall.
"What a tumult!" he says. "Come here often?"
"No," I shout. "Only when people visit."

I take him to the Olive Garden for lunch.
They step on his cape. Now he's drinking heavy,
spilling red wine on his puffy hat with balls.

He won't eat anything. I apologize.
He throws the salad bowl across the dining room.
"This is ridiculous," he says, crossing his arms.

I love the library. I take him to the library.
"What is this farce?" he demands, cigarette
hanging from his mouth. I raise my hands

to the bookshelves in a grand gesture of possibility.
He throws his head back and tromps out with great pomp.
Outside, I find him smoking by the fountain.

His cape is over his head.
He's insulting passing women.
"Where are the bulls?" he shouts to no one in particular.

"Where is death and beauty?" he screams.
"Back off freak!" says a scampering woman.
I hand him an ice cream cone.

He looks up at me as cloud shadow passes over his face.
Finally, he takes my confection and breaks down weeping.
I don't know what he's crying about. This ice cream is good.

How Our Living Room Became a Cemetery

Ted was so old he turned into a tombstone.
He wasn't exactly dead, not in the rotting-in-the-ground,
not in the worms-through-his-eyes kind of way,
just the not-moving-your-limbs-much kind of way.

We could tell he was still alive
because his epitaph would change all the time
and didn't have the usual sentimental rigmarole about
"Husband, Father" or "Loving, Dedicated" et cetera.

The carved inscription would say things
like "Can you get me a beer?" or
"Is that bacon I smell?"

We didn't much mind Ted being a tombstone.
In fact, his epitaphs carried more weight
than any words Ted ever said.

But then the neighbors thought we had buried a body
in our living room. They wanted to call the police.
We tried to explain.
"You think if we buried a body in our living room
we'd put up a tombstone?"

It didn't help that the tombstone suddenly read
"You're a moron." The neighbors didn't find that funny.
"Look, not only did you kill someone,
you insult him on the tombstone. What kind of sick people are you?"

So it wasn't long before our entire house was destroyed
by the police as they searched for the body.
And poor Ted was buried in the evidence room downtown,
left to quietly change his epitaph in the dark
for God knows how long.

Heaven

I don't know if I want all this fog and white light.
I think I would prefer it to be more like walking upstairs from the
    basement,
listening to the laugh track on the television grow louder.
I would want the smell of turkey with potatoes and gravy.
Maybe a fire in the fireplace. That's right, I said
a fire in heaven. And when I reached the top of the stairs
I would want my wife to be laughing at me
because I'm wearing one of those standard Jesus robes and no one
    else is.
I hope heaven will look like a furniture store.
I can't wait to hear her say, "Try this couch.
No, try this one. Wow. They're all great!"
All the while the citizens of heaven are staring at me because I'm the
    only one in a robe.
But that's all right because I would put my palm up in that Jesus way
so everyone would know I was friendly.

Shelving

I bought some shelving the other day
and installed it in my garage. I lined it
with blow up rafts, paint cans,
gardening tools, a car battery,
some foam coolers, some basketballs,
a few cheap red toolboxes,
and on the wall next to it
a poster of a woman in a bikini
holding a cordless power drill.

Why stop there?
I put some shelving up in my car.
I took out the back seat and built a small library.
Every book was about walking
down the street. If I felt attuned
to my fellow pedestrians,
I would throw a book at them as I drove by.
Of course, it amazed them—
I always had the right book for the occasion.

I was so excited.
I built shelving onto myself.
People would store parts of their lives on me.
However, it was difficult to move around
with the burden of history, keeping track
yet still moving on.

Folding Chairs

Like folding chairs
we find that we too
have folded at times and set ourselves against walls
after being used for a while
after the company has left
and the act of doing the dishes seems almost celebratory.

This is the moment we are comfortable
in our simple acts:
hanging a shirt on a hook,
standing at a window, watching snow
fill the grass.

The vacuumed space of the floor
seems a possibility,
as if everything we are
will have a purpose soon,

even if it's simply sitting down
at a late hour to listen
to one heart in the body's closet
unfolding and folding
for a thousand visitations.

Gentle Majesty

I am ashamed.
Part of me wants to go whaling.
I want to wear rain gear and carry a harpoon.
It's horrible
but part of me wants to sink the harpoon to the hilt
and feel blood from the blowhole spewing over my face.
I want to eat clam chowder with Queequeg.
Call me Scottshmael.

But as part of my suburban training
I know whaling is cruel
and whales are majestic animals,
so silent, gentle, and beautiful.

So I decided to harpoon my couch instead.
I donned all the yellow whaling gear.
I even brought a small boat into the living room.
I had the harpoon raised when my wife came home.

"Don't do it! Don't do it!" she cried.
"You can't stop me, landlubber," I answered.
"It's a brand new couch. It's defenseless.
Look at its gentle majesty."

I dropped the harpoon in the boat.
The couch was beautiful—purple, over-stuffed.
It was the nicest thing in the house.
"I want to harpoon something.
Is there anything that doesn't have gentle majesty anymore?"
"No. No," she said. "The world
is full of gentle majesty. Look around."

The cat was gnawing at itself.
The sink teemed with food-covered dishes.
Empty liquor bottles littered the floor.

Who could argue? Such beauty.
We finished off the evening on the couch,
bathed in the blue light of gentle majesty,
eating popcorn, watching *Barnaby Jones* reruns,
our feet comfortably sailing along on the boat's gunwales.

Can't Sleep

Sometimes my son or daughter
is asleep on the couch.
Sometimes I am.

Sometimes I wake up
and my wife
has already taken my spot.

We trade places
several times
throughout the night.

Our couch is a good couch
and receives all equally.
It doesn't ask dumb questions.

Death must be something
like a clouded room
with a purple couch in it.

You fall asleep
for a little while,
then trade with someone else.

Dying Wishes

"How do you want to be buried?"
she asks, off hand, one night in bed.
Perhaps I should have been suspicious
but instead was suddenly in love.

"Well, if you really want to know," I say,
"I would love to be shot out of a cannon
from the top of Beacon Rock,
that 1000 ft. monolith of towering stone
in the scenic Columbia River Gorge,
while competing Junior High School marching bands
simultaneously play "Battle Hymn of the Republic"
and that song that begins
"I believe in miracles" by Hot Chocolate
and a small group of family and friends
in tuxedoes and cocktail dresses
sit nearby on wooden chairs sipping 25-year-old
single malt scotch, everyone holding
on his lap a small folio of my poems
sprinkled with thousand dollar perfume,
all expertly written out in calligraphy
on handmade Italian paper lined with gold leaf—
each poem handpicked to individual tastes and life stage needs.

"Where the fuck am I going to get a cannon?" she says.
And in this instance I realized my earlier feeling of love
was but a speck compared to the love
exploding within me, because now I can clearly see her
with gray hair, wearing a cardigan,
driving an old white Crown Victoria, going
from Target to Walmart to Circuit City,
desperately looking for a cannon
while my corpse rots away in the back seat.

"How about I just roll your dead body
off the roof and into the front yard? Deal?"
"It's a deal," I say, because delirious in love
I can think of nothing else
as she kisses me and turns off the lights.

How Good It Feels to Die

I was buried yesterday.
Yes, maybe I should have been more careful.
I was taking a stroll through the graveyard
and this coffin was just nestled there in the ground,
and you know it was one of those sleepy fall days
where the sun is soft and slants in
from the right on a cool carpet of air.

Maybe it's those leaves . . . the shuffling
through the graveyard . . . the whispering
that always turns me into a baby, says,
"Just take a nap here before dinner time."
Hey, I can't help it if somebody left the lid off.
You can't leave this fluffy softness just lying around
in a muddy graveyard.

I'd been writing poems all day and trying to
come up with new metaphors for clouds,
so many metaphors that it felt like
each cloud was sticking a thousand white asses at me.
And you'd be surprised how comfy a coffin is.
I mean, some dead people really have it made.
I imagined this is how lunchmeat feels
in between two pieces of soft white bread.

I don't know how long I was there but
I woke up in the dark trying to roll over.
I'm not that stupid. I had my cell phone. I knew where I was.
You'd be amazed what great reception the dead get.
"Hi, honey, it's me.
Yes, I'm at Lone Fir."
"Oh, not again," she always says.

"Yep, I'm calling from the grave.
It's the fresh dirt by the big oak near the road.
Call me back if you can't find it."
And then I wait
and the best part is always the wait,
snuggled inside the dark,
listening for shovel taps,
knowing those who love you
are on their way to bring you back.

CHAMPAGNE
Côte de Vancouver
BRUT

Scott Poole is the house poet for *Live Wire!*, a weekly radio variety show on Oregon Public Broadcasting that airs throughout the Pacific Northwest and is currently expanding to Public Broadcasting radio stations across the U.S. in cities such as Boston and Cleveland. He also was the founding director of *Get Lit!*, the Spokane, Washington, book festival, and *Wordstock*, the Portland, Oregon, book festival. Currently he is a software developer and lives in Vancouver, Washington.

Also by Scott Poole

The Cheap Seats
Hiding from Salesmen

The author gratefully acknowledges *Sugar House Review*, *Redactions*, *NOÖ Journal*, *Slow Trains*, and *Inertia* where some of these poems originally appeared.